The Beautiful Golden Butterfly

Copyright 2013 by David J. Hastings

First Edition – December 2013

ISBN

978-0-9936344-0-6 (Paperback)

978-0-9936344-1-3 (eBook)

All rights reserved.

Except for brief quotations utilized in book reviews

or commentary, no part of this book may be used or

reproduced in any fashion whatsoever without express written permission.

For additional information email:

thebeautifulgoldenbutterfly@gmail.com

Dedicated

To   Lydia Burchell

"The Doubt Doctor"

And all

   trapped in cocoons

      of limiting beliefs...

May you find the courage

   to re-choose living unfettered

   and

         Fly Free

Once upon a time...

there was

a

Beautiful

Golden

Butterfly

Unfortunately

She did not

know

She was

She had built herself

a very small

and

very confining

cocoon

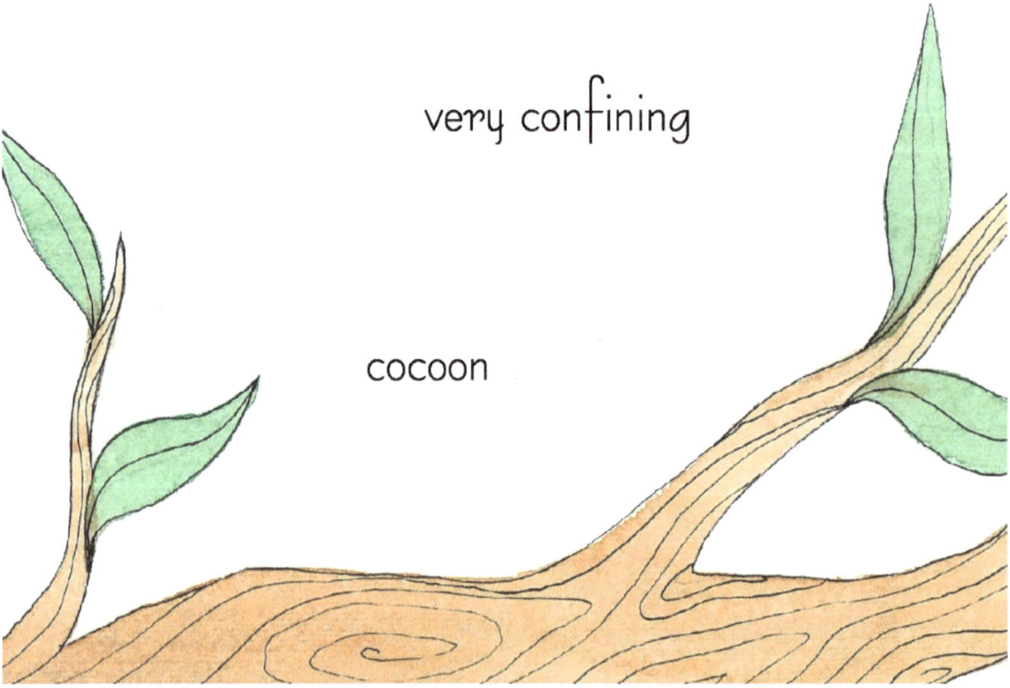

From this tiny place

She was

unable

to see

her magnificence

SO small it was

From within

She tried to understand

what reason there could be

for her existence

She tried peering out

but was unable to see well

as she had built the

cocoons shell

so very thick and secure

Feeling very unworthy

She was much too fearful

to venture out or even

have passers-by notice her

Feeling trapped and alone

She was unable to see her true self…

She was slowly dying inside

At times,

    tearfully and desperately,

She tried to escape

        but with each try

her cocoon world

    seemed to become

even smaller

limiting her all the more

Ultimately

this little world

was all she allowed

herself to believe in

Day after day

She made wishes

    for the courage to escape

        to go out there

Do good

    Be noticed

        Appreciated

           Beautiful

              Useful

and feel worthy

As wishes go...

one day a man spotted

this lone cocoon with a

Beautiful Golden Butterfly

mysteriously trapped inside...

Assuming... by her sad expression...

She felt unimportant

He asked

If he could stay a while

He told her true beauty

always starts within

He called her

"Beautiful Beautiful"

for both her shrouded inside beauty

and

her obvious outside beauty...

for this is what

he truly saw

She was very unsure of him...

She could not think of any reason

why this person

should take

any genuine notice

of a plain cocoon

or a trapped

butterfly

Her emotions were very fragile...

tormented by her perceived plight

She was unable to speak at first

She was full of self-doubt

She felt completely unacceptable...

She was as disbelieving in herself as anyone can be

This man softly exclaimed,

But can you not see

You are a

Beautiful Golden

Butterfly

Shining brightly

through this confinement

You have built?"

"Why did you build it",

he queried?

"To hide" she replied,

..."even though that is not

what I really want"

After speaking with

this man for a time

She began to recognize

Thoughts

She carried about herself

were incorrect...

She was valuable...

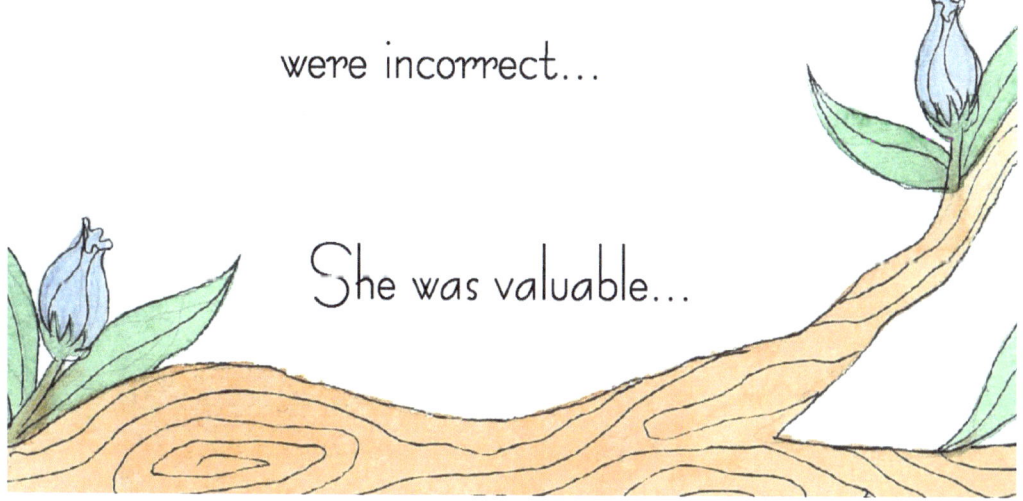

Bit by bit

She picked away

pieces of the cocoon...

very cautiously at first...

As the opening slowly widened

allowing a clear outside view

She began to believe a new way of living

was possible for her

She began feeling acceptable

As the last too familiar pieces

of the encircling cocoon

were about to be shed

She began to speak freely

for the first time…

Realizing this man believed in her…

even when fettered

inside her limiting cocoon…

She took a chance

and broke totally free

To her excited amazement

She suddenly understood…

  now unrestricted by the cocoon…

She could spread her wings

            For the first time

She was indeed

    what he had said all along…

  a

    Beautiful Golden Butterfly

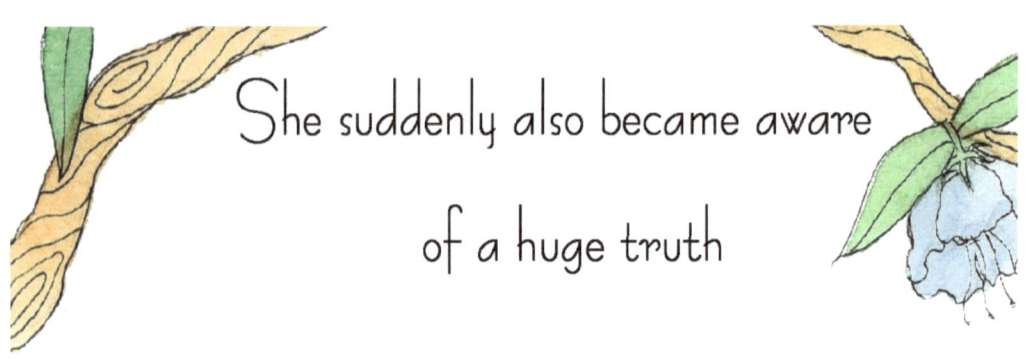

She suddenly also became aware

of a huge truth

She had falsely thought of herself

badly

for a very long time...

Now...

realizing this

she craved to fly free

and fulfill her dreams

This man

       did not want

    to capture

        Beautiful Golden Butterfly

Only enjoy

    witnessing the start

      of her new journey…

The beginnings

of her discovering

supressed individual wonders

and

all the marvels out there…

She was truly

Ready to fly away

Although very sad

    for losing his new love

He was very happy

    completely believing

Beautiful Golden Butterfly...

    with her new-found

appreciation of herself...

    would do wondrous things

He was filled with joy

She had come to appreciate her uniqueness

...and now...

By correctly believing in her own competence and capability...

She was ready to experience everything possible...and

Find her True Destiny

www.ingramcontent.com/pod-product-compliance
Lightning Source LLC
Chambersburg PA
CBHW041753040426
42446CB00001B/19